THE
LUMBERJACK'S
DOVE

THE LUMBERJACK'S DOVE

A POEM

GENNAROSE NETHERCOTT

ecco

An Imprint of HarperCollins*Publishers*

HarperCollins books may be purchased for educational, business, or sales promotional use. For information please e-mail the Special Markets Department at SPsales@harpercollins.com.

FIRST EDITION

Designed by Suet Yee Chong

Library of Congress Cataloging-in-Publication Data has been applied for.

ISBN 978-0-06-285367-7

18 19 20 21 22 LSC 10 9 8 7 6 5 4 3 2 1

For my father, Michael Nethercott,

who, all my life long, fed me on the silver apples
of the moon, the golden apples of the sun.

THE
LUMBERJACK'S
DOVE

PART 1

It's the same old story:

A lumberjack loses a hand to his own axe. The hand becomes a dove. The hand tries to fly away but the lumberjack catches it beneath his shoe. You know this story. The lumberjack ties one end of a string to the hand & the other end to his belt. Then the lumberjack walks out of the forest, the airborne hand fluttering along behind.

———————————

There are three rules of storytelling:

1. Only tell a story if you have to. If you can survive without telling it, keep mum.

2. A story is a two-way mirror. Don't think the characters cannot see you. It's safest to assume they can always see you, & they know exactly where you live.

3. The purest way to speak truth is by lying.

Slow it down. This is how a hand morphs as it abandons the limb. First, carpal bones lose their weight. Fingers hollow into piccolos. Next, lumbricales twist & re-form. The ulnar nerve & radial artery elongate through the bottom of the wrist, elbow bend & harden, grow talons. The thumb sheds from flesh to bone, bone to beak. Carves into point & split. Feathers bristle up from skin; an afterthought. Now for the hard part.

Now for the hard part. Flight, o wild ghost, anti-burial. Tendons weave into fans. Delicate, so easy to tangle. Uncurl from the palm into wings, all wet & spooked by newness.

Watch them discover their strength, accordioning until the new body, severed from the old body, lifts itself into the air & flies towards a nearby branch.

Lumberjack clutches the absent space at the end of his arm. He looks up at the dove, who in turn, looks back at him, already forgetting it was ever anything but sovereign.

Stories are best in threes—Lumberjack: The abandoned. Hand: The abandoner. Axe: Means of abandonment. No matter who you are, all you are ever doing is leaving or being left or acting as the impetus to leave.

Again, & again, & again.
This is every story.
This is the trinity.

It's a betrayal, really. A man is born with this body. Everyone tells him it's his. They call it by his name. They pet this body & clothe this body & teach him that this body, it's with him forever.

———

A Portrait: Arms twinned in blue flannel, rolled to the elbow. Blue veins like garter snakes. Freckles dusting the collarbone & nose & throat. Pink scar check-marked on the upper lip from a BB gun misfire. Rag in the back pocket. A firm sense of direction. A restlessness.

Lumberjack starts his pickup truck. He keeps the windows closed as he drives & the dove floats up to bounce against the glass. The road is slick with rain. Worms boil up from the earth. Now there is a shirt tied around the wound, the fabric growing sticky & dark with ache. A bootlace becomes a tourniquet. A terrible yank settles in the basement of his heart, the lowest stair.

Some men have a gift for controlling which way a tree will fall. They spit snuff into undergrowth to interpret like tea leaves. They light brushfires just to speak to the smoke. When a trunk drops, it could almost be mistaken for bowing.

When Axe & Lumberjack touch, whole forests die for them.

Axe has loved often & by "loved," I mean she has cleaved many pieces off many bodies.

———————

Lumberjack drives towards the witch doctor or he drives to the E.R. depending on who's telling the story, & depending on if the storyteller is a liar.

In the truck bed, Axe watches the sky peel towards dusk. Onwards, they drive & drive & drive.

PART II

In the version of the story where Lumberjack goes to the E.R., a receptionist asks him to fill out a form with his name. He writes down all of them. One for every telling.

———————

Hospital Inpatient Form

Reason for Visit: My hand is trying to fly. Something separated my hand & myself & now I want to reclaim what is mine. I want myself reunited with myself. I want my hand to shrivel without me. I want.

Remember, there are infinite stories about separation. By infinite stories, that is to say that there is this story, & only this story, told many different ways. Sometimes the hand is not a hand but a sweetheart or a daughter or a house on fire. Anything can be part of oneself & anything can be taken away. Sometimes the truck is a fishing boat or a Boeing 747 or a blocked telephone number. Sometimes the abandoned never makes it free of the forest.

Quick, go to the blue chairs & the wall poster of a skeleton. Stacks of flyers: *Quit Smoking Today; You & Your Pregnancy; Living with Arthritis.* Names & dates & numbers on a form don't matter when your hand is affixed by a piece of twine. Details can come later.

Posters of skeletons are far less motivational than actual skeletons. When it comes to heeding a color Xerox or heeding the dead, the dead always win. The dead win every game they ever play.

———————

There is only one other patient in the waiting room. She is mostly bald, with a few bright patches stealing up from the scalp. *I cut it all off,* she says, *but it was a mistake.*

Will the doctor stitch it back on? asks Lumberjack. He knows little of what doctors can & cannot do. He knows little of the rules of removal & replacement.

The woman pets the mass of her own hair, piled in her lap. It growls, nips at her thumb. Once a part of the body is removed, it belongs to itself.

Her head catches light like a new sun. The hair in her lap smolders like underbrush burned to clear a work site. She's beautiful. She looks like she was just born, but not for the first time.

Later: The woman was called in hours ago
& hasn't come out yet. Maybe this is a
good sign. Maybe this is a terrible sign. The
dove is asleep on Lumberjack's shoulder.
Little breaths. He wonders where his hand
found its own pair of lungs, its own tongue,
its own plumage, its own tiny heart
shivering like a water droplet about to
release the spigot.

—————

Simple tasks spring leaks when your grip is
winged. A bottle shatters in its journey to
the mouth. Handwriting adopts wide
swoops as if caught on a thermal. It
becomes impossible to trace the map of a
darling's skin, or dial the telephone, or hold
a soupspoon. Instead, your hand will preen
by the open window. Lift out of reach.
Abandon the duties for which it was built.

Here, read an old issue of *Highlights* magazine. Read *Woman's Day*. 60 ways to bake a quiche. 55 new ab workouts. 23 spells to make your lovers bow to you, dirty their knees, call you almighty. 10 sigils to etch into the sand. 4 ways to live forever. You will live forever.

You will live forever.

PART III

In the version of the story in which the wounded man goes to the witch doctor, he drives for three full days & nights. He cauterizes the wound with the truck's cigarette lighter. He runs out of gas, but somehow, the truck keeps on going.

Like all major U.S. highways, I-91 functions as a direct trail to the witch doctor. All you have to do is drive straight. You can tell you are near when the radio static is replaced with birdcalls.

Ten miles to go; the truck windows lick with cracks like a river map. Seven; rust bubbles along the undercarriage. Six miles; the rear left tire sprouts a puncture, leaving air to wail free like a spirit fleeing a corpse. Four & three-quarter miles from the witch doctor, & the engine sprints into flames. The doors are drawn & quartered from the sockets. Three crows land on the hood & dip their beaks into the oil tank as if drinking from a streambed.

When you enter unknown territory with only one hand, choices must be made— leave it open & ready to catch? Or carry a weapon?

Lumberjack pulls Axe from the truck bed & into his surviving hand. He may need her.

Many people think of Axe as beautiful.
There must be some allure to danger. They
love her in that golden way reserved for
the untrustworthy. When she disassembles
them, they almost seem grateful.

All men want is to love someone with
better things to do than love them back.

The Blade: Shark fin & steel. Wedging from thin to fat like a pie slice. Shine on a shirttail until light twists like a fun-house mirror. Expect to see Axe, but instead, find your own reflection. Funny, the unexpected places you appear—in a tool; a bird; a storyteller's throat.

———————

It is important to note that Lumberjack lost his dominant right hand.

Curiosity is a terrible elixir. A love potion. Enough to make a man drunk. To prompt him to swing an axe with his weaker fist, just for the sport of it. The foreman often chastised him for these experiments. But it only takes one mistake. One folly.

The weak becomes the only.

Now, the left hand carries Axe along the road. To wield a weapon in a clumsy limb is not an exercise in protection. It is an exercise in feeling less alone.

The dove has no choice but to follow. There is nowhere to go but forward.

The horizon swallows the highway. Tarmac stretches onwards, flat & straight & blistered with sun. On either side of the road, barbed wire is nailed between wood posts. Atop each post is an animal skull. There are hundreds of posts & hundreds of skulls. Rabbit, gull, deer, bull. Then the unrecognizable: One with black antlers webbing from cheekbones. Another with an eye socket in the center of the forehead. Another with no mouth.

A mouthless jaw implies the following:

a. The creature did not eat.

b. The creature did eat, but nothing that could be ingested traditionally. Not the sort of food one can touch.

c. The creature had a mouth once, which at some point, the witch took away.

& at once, a house. There, in the cornfield, just twenty yards away. It is avoiding shadow in a most curious manner. It ripples the way heat ripples against desert.

Roof alive with prairie grass & sod. Stained glass windows. The house squats on seven wooden legs, knee-bent & spidered. A rope ladder uncurls like a fern. Bone chimes hang above the door & sing, though there is no wind.

Crows blacken the ground in front of the house. The dove is a pinprick in the center of a great dark pupil. It is the only star alive.

Can corn go on forever? Can a house be alive? Can a life be a house? Approach. How do you climb a rope ladder with a single hand? Approach. Stop asking questions & expecting answers.

———————

There are three rules of storytelling:

1. Be careful what stories you tell.

2. All stories told will manifest & become real.

3. Sometimes a story doesn't make sense. Sometimes it will contradict itself, but be true, anyway.

On the precipice, the dove won't stop beating itself against the door. Six, seven, eight, nine. Muscle memory—this was its duty once. The knocking. Twelve, thirteen. Some knowing is left. Some notion of what came before. Fifteen, sixteen, seventeen. Memory = colliding with the same barriers repeatedly & demanding different results. Or no, that's insanity. No, it is certainly both.

—————

The door opens.

So Lumberjack enters. He enters the house the way he might enter a woman—driven by a need to be made whole.

This is the part of the telling when the storyteller pauses. You remember your grandmother or your sister's best friend or the bus driver quieting & turning away. Your grandmother gets a glass of water. Your sister's best friend decides to put on a cooler dress, & you watch her change in the corner, peripherally. The bus driver unwraps a piece of Big Red chewing gum. Sun catches on the paper, silver like a fish. Suspense. You are a mantis caught beneath a cup. You powerless thing.

PART IV

A pause in a story is not a chance for you to rest. There is no rest. It is simply a turning of the head, towards another possible outcome, happening simultaneously & constantly.

The story is always being told somewhere.

At the hospital, Lumberjack is still waiting & still bleeding. The dove begins to mince magazines in its beak. It gathers the bits into a pile. So far, it has accrued a heap of twelve shredded tabloids.

The dove starts to pluck at a tatter on the upholstery. *Stop that*, Lumberjack says, & startles. He is talking to part of himself. That can't be right. If you speak to a bird & that bird is capable of listening, it must be its own & not a part of the speaker's body. Body parts cannot listen. They cannot collect fabric scraps because they have no motive of their own.

———————

The dove ignores the demand. It weaves thread into magazine clippings. It dampens the paper with filtered water from the cooler & begins to mold. First, it uses its feet to pluck the collection into a mound. Then it settles its body into the small hill, tamping the center down into a bowl.

The dove is building a nest.

A Portrait: Fragile. Lacelike. Loose enough
for light to pass through. Better hold breath
to avoid scattering. Mottled with stray
down & red ringlets. Swirled like a
hurricane, quiet as the storm's eye.

———————

Lumberjack considers kicking it to show
the dove who's in charge. But o, there is
some lovely music to it. It's more intricate
than anything he ever could have built.

In a moment, the delay will end. We will leave the magazines & pamphlets & water cooler behind. We will enter the doctor's office. Some fate or another will present itself. But for now, time is distracted. It is examining a dove's nest on an emergency waiting room floor.

———————

Time does this, sometimes—pauses to appreciate an object of beauty. It grows so enamored that it forgets to move forward. A meadow or a clavicle or a painting might be the secret to immortality. Enough loveliness, & time will stop altogether.

The doctor will see you now.

The dove is curled in its nest. Just a tug on
the twine would evict the bird. Lumberjack
does not do this. Instead, he slips his good
hand beneath the little home & lifts it. He
holds it like a newborn, close to his body,
as he follows a nurse into the operating
room.

Today, home is a thing he can hold, as long
as he doesn't hold too tight. A place that
balances in an open hand. This will not
happen again. Home is not in the habit of
repeating itself.

This is how it goes—wait & wait & wait & nothing happens & then all of a sudden the whole hospital is singing.

———————————

The surgical technician wraps the dove with moistened gauze & floats it in a plastic bag of ice water. The anesthesiologist inserts an intravenous line.

Lumberjack is alone in the forest. Trees are telling him to sleep. A doe finds a bullet in her belly. A red-tailed hawk coughs up a cradle of bones.

Anesthetics discover the brain. The man on the operating table remembers even less of his name now. He is sawdust in the wind.

———————

If he has a name, it doesn't matter. A name is a name is a name. A lover is a lover is a prize is a story.

Every time the storyteller says the word "lover," replace it with the word "self." The word "self," replace with "lover." Dizzying, isn't it? When vertigo sets in, plant saplings. Replace "lover" with "cedar" or "dogwood." Replace "self" with "poplar" or "sugar maple." Keep swapping out words until no one is left but the forest.

The dove rattles its body against gauze. It can see its nest, there in the crook of the sleeping man's elbow. It needs the nest back. One, two, three, it bats against the inside of the plastic bag. Four, five, knock, knock, knock, its home is in someone else's arms. Six, seven, eight. Grip slacks with sleep & the nest falls. Nine, ten, the bag punctures at beak point. Water flows out in ribbons.

Living creatures believe they own something as soon as they love it. They refuse to believe otherwise, no matter how many times a beloved vanishes.

The surgeon needs to know now: Can the hand be saved? So the technician unwraps the dove—cool & silvered with wet, wing tips sagged, its eyes galaxies, its heart a land mine. The dove's wings are spread open by blue rubber gloves. It is laid on its back. Tackboard slides beneath it. Then, with two soft pops, one through each wing, it is stapled to the table.

I'll make this quick & honest.

The surgeon inserts a scalpel into the dove's trachea & slits down towards the pelvis. The dove's stomach grins open. Its lungs go dark. It wants for nothing.

———————

Back in the truck bed, Axe feels a shift. It begins to snow. The snow falls directly onto the truck & nowhere else in the parking lot. The snow is not snow. The snowflakes are feathers & they are falling faster. They fill the truck bed until Axe is buried & gone & reaching up for a surface she cannot touch.

If the surgeon expected to find a hand within the bird, still intact, he was disappointed. He should have known that not everything is a mask or a box containing something else. Some things just are.

The primary surgeon, the technician, & the anesthesiologist do not read entrails to divine the future. Medical practitioners are not trained in haruspicy. Had they been, the liver would stretch & squeeze like a concertina. It would sing aloud their descendants' names & count their freckles & scars & mimic their voices. It would tell how the descendants' lives would end—in passenger seats, in factories, on operating tables not unlike this one.

But the surgeon, the technician, & the anesthesiologist are sworn to science. The liver stays silent. All they have is a dead bird pinned to a tabletop.

———————

What they do see: A gizzard, small intestine, pancreas, crop, heart, buccal cavity, esophagus, & just past the ribs, an egg.

Tiny egg, pallid & smooth. Tight as a dime. Little pill, little lightbulb. Translucent with incompletion, not yet ready for laying. It is the centerpiece on a splayed altar.

When the patient awakens, pain electrifies his arm. He looks at the hand, but the hand is not there. Skin is stretched over bone & stitched in place. Pain floats outside the body, just beyond the wrist. It is a haunted pain, built not of what is, but of what should be.

Then he sees the dove, flayed like a satsuma. His hand is never coming back.

———————————

We leave the operating room. Here are pamphlets on how to care for the stump as it heals. In the bag with the pamphlets are a tube of antibacterial jelly, fifty yards of gauze, & a bottle of painkillers. The surgeon apologizes that more could not be done.

Take this:
An open shoe box & within the shoe box is
the nest & within the nest is the egg, alive
& brittle & holy as a new planet.

———————————

This story was written a long, long time
ago, before car keys or replantation surgery
or radios were invented. It was written for
you & it was written generations before
your birth. A story as true as this one tosses
time over its shoulder like a fistful of salt.
A story as true as this knows what is to
come.

PART V

The witch doctor: Cut her & count one hundred tree rings. Then the light shifts, & she is twenty-two & beautiful. Hair of razor wire & ivy, braided in a wreath. Fingernails sharpened to points. She will unwrap a person with an index finger & tinker—she, a clocksmith; the patient, a pocket watch.

———

Lumberjack leans Axe against the wall. Proof that loyalty is easy to put aside. Simply set it down & walk away, towards someone new.

He grabs the dove from air like a peach from a branch & slams it down on the tabletop. *Fix it.*

He is arrogant, because he thinks he is owed a lot. Maybe he is. Maybe he isn't. It's difficult to say what any one person is entitled to.

———

The bird squirms against the table. Its little pulse is throbbing. Let go, let go, let go.

Never, thinks Lumberjack. *Never.*

I will never let you go.
I will never let you go.

The witch puts a kettle on to boil. She stirs nightshade into a china cup & lets it steep, takes a sip.

Everything has the ability to help, or harm, depending on how it's used, & how thirsty you are when you swallow it.

Her pupils: Hollow as a chapel, black as plums.

To be a proper houseguest, you must never leave your clothes around the house. You mustn't give gin to the cat. Avoid bleeding on the furniture. If possible, do not touch the furniture at all. Do not touch the floor or walls. Leave no marks. No stray hair on a pillowcase. No breath condensing on windowpanes. Take up no space. Never let the hostess know you are there. This assures that when you leave, you do not leave a gap.

The cruelest act a person can commit is to leave a gap.

We have been waiting for seven years, or five minutes, or not at all, or three days, or have watched western civilization rise & fall on the television in the corner.

———————

There are three rules of storytelling:

1. Stories don't care about your prior appointments. They make their own schedule. They are not service minded. If a story doesn't make you wait, it isn't worth a damn.

2. Every story is about you.

3. Never ask a story for answers, or it will swallow you alive in punishment.

All right, says the witch doctor. *Let me have a look.*

————————

& Lumberjack holds out his stump & she unwraps the fabric around it & pours bourbon on the wound & the wounded hisses into steam & returns to his body & now the stump is clean & raw & ready.

Most storytellers aren't sure where to go from here, because none of them have met a witch doctor. In general, storytellers stick to what they know. The witch doctor is largely unknowable, because when you look at her she seems to scatter & re-form. She is only clear in periphery. So the storyteller improvises. Says something like this:

. . . & the witch doctor spreads a thistle salve across the dove's back & the dove becomes a hand again.

or

. . . she gives the dove a thimble of blood to swallow, the dove becomes a hand again.

or

. . . she licks the stump, which sprouts new palm, fingertips, bone . . .

This telling is not like the others. I know the witch doctor. Other storytellers are charlatans & not to be trusted. Watch your wallet & your keys around them. Watch your quiet heart.

———————

This is how it happened:

Now show me your good hand.
He holds it out.

The witch doctor sets a sewing needle to flesh. Along his lifeline she stitches streambeds gone dry. Thread becomes woodlands. Seeds are buried & saplings embroider up towards the sun. Boys are born among the silk. They learn to hold weapons & to unbutton a dress in the dark & they learn to hew the forest at the waist. They learn to claim what may or may not be theirs to claim. The witch doctor sews & sews & as she does, forests & boys rise & fall.

———————

Reclamation Spell

Ingredients:
One wooden bowl
One copper bowl
One clay bowl
The abandoned
The abandoner
The means of abandonment
Three matches & a strike pad
An incantation

The witch plucks a tail feather from the dove; scrapes a splinter off Axe with a paring knife; takes up Lumberjack's sewn hand. Each, she places in one of the bowls. She drops a lit match on all three—a quick singe.

Incantations can be written on diner napkins, sheepskin parchment, envelopes, in the margins of instructional manuals, or in the dust on a back windshield. The words vary—could be a poem, or an address. Could be a hymnal.

This incantation is a number.

108.0

108.0

A mourning dove's average body
temperature.

Peak human body temperature before
death.

A radio coordinate.

––––––––––––

The radio switches itself on. Axe wakes up
in the corner. Her favorite folk song is
playing. When they were partners,
Lumberjack would sing it as he seized her
body. She would collide with the tree in
time to the rhythm. At the height of the
chorus, her darling's voice would rise &
rise & then, in clean harmony, the log
would split open like a mouth.

Come all you shanty boys
take up the hatchet blade
& as you lay the woodlands low
sing out this serenade.
Hemlocks do not die with ease
but stumble out of life
like drunkards dragging off their boots
to bed beside their wives.
There is a changing moment
when the spirit is set free,
when a man becomes a body,
& when wood replaces tree.
O shanty boys with axes high,
you know this instant well
for you alone have felled the trunks
& watched the sap dispel.
Yes you alone have seen the way
leviathans may fall
& rot upon the forest floor
as one day will we all.

Axe is up & dancing. She is boogieing around the house, knocking over pots & dishes, scuffing up the floorboards, leaving splinters. She is crooning along & her blade is glowing red-hot. *my oh my, what a song, what a song, what a time it was! remember, remember? the way the trees bowed to us? they must have really loved us, loved us to the point of dying* & she runs to Lumberjack & grabs his only hand & pulls it to her with a thwack.

A clean cut.

———————

It's the same old story:
A lumberjack loses a hand to his own axe. You know this story. The hand does not become a dove. It does not become anything but severed. The hand lies in a clay bowl until someone drops a lit match on it, & it turns to ash.

Meanwhile, the dove nuzzles against the right stump where it once belonged.

Slow it down. This is how a hand returns to the arm. First, wings retract into shoulder. The urge for flight brushes loose like dust. Feathers molt. Then vertebrae stretch into finger bones. Knuckles bulge & crack. The beak softens, twists into thumbprint. Next, belly fuses with wrist. Calluses return to the palm. All is as it was.

———————————

Sacrifice is a requirement. The world rests on a Libra's scale. For new saplings to root, others must fall. To walk towards one home, you must turn on another. To nurture the right hand, you must neglect the left.

Lumberjack doesn't rejoice. All he can feel is the new screech on his left arm. A sudden absence. He doesn't care that all he begged for has returned. He doesn't thank the witch doctor. & it is not until later, as he walks down the highway back to his pickup, Axe pinned under his arm, that he notices something new in his closed fist. Firm & warm.

An egg.

PART VI

You probably have a favorite version of the story. When you first heard it, many years ago, you knew right away which of the two you believed. As you aged, your trust redirected whenever you met a milestone— the first time you hurt another person; the first time you were drunk; the moment you bought a plane ticket away; the last time you glimpsed yourself in a mirror or a blade. You can't recall which version you started with.

This is where the two reconverge:

Lumberjack drives back towards the woodlands. He stops to fill the tank at a gas station off exit 17 & fumbles with the nozzle. There are many simple maneuvers to relearn. Twisting the gas cap, extracting his wallet, pulling the trigger . . .

Gasoline thickens the air, & for a moment he forgets to mourn.

—————

He drives & drives & drives. He puts the egg in the ashtray, where it won't break. It must be lovely in there, he thinks. No light, no sound, just musk & the notion of speed.

Axe doesn't believe in folktales. She believes in her own precision. The wind casts acorns & leaves into the pickup bed. *I taught your fathers how to love,* Axe sings to them, *& by love, I mean to be felled, sliced to lumber, & reassembled into a new body.* She isn't sure what she means when she says this, but it feels like the truth.

——————————

Lumberjack parks at the forest's edge. He transfers the egg to his pocket & walks into the woods. Eventually, he makes his way to a tree with a gash in the side—an incomplete job. The bark is black with blood. A trail marker. A memory.

There are three rules of storytelling:

1. All stories end with a beginning.

2. Every character is a shapeshifter. Every object is a seed.

3. The purest way to speak truth is by lying.

Lumberjack digs a hole at the trunk's base, three inches wide & six inches deep. Then he cares for the egg the only way he knows how: He plants it.

What is truth?

Here: You are holding an axe head, polished as a looking glass. Your cheek is familiar in the strange, silver light. Your brow. Your lip. Your heart.

It is not really you, of course. Only a reflection. & yet . . .

Were the mirror untrue, you would not recognize this reflection as your own.

(So too functions a story.)

Wait three days & three nights. Dampen the soil. Feed it river water. Tell it fables— those of crows & forgiveness, of beautiful women once known, of letters sent & received.

All night, the moon grants amnesty. Wolves do not tarry for prey. The forest spits shadows at other loggermen to draw them into labyrinths. The sycamore breathes in & out forty times. & then, at last, comes dawn.

A hemlock tree has grown from the egg. Red paint flickers along the bark. Gold thread & newsprint bud the branches. Silhouetted against the morning sky, each bough is heavy, so bountiful as to drag towards the ground, fat with a most peculiar fruit.

A Portrait: Hung from the bough like ripe peaches. Five-fingered & reaching. The hands grow in clusters, one upon the next. Soft in their newness—no callus, no splinter, no burn. Opening & closing, clasping each other, widening palms to catch beginning rain. O there is so much to hold.

————————

When you discover an ending to this story, it will not be on the lips of a storyteller. I have no lock for this door. You may come upon it in a rain gutter or a pulled-tooth gap. You may find it in an aviary. You may glimpse it in your headlights on a midnight highway. A shadow. An atlas. A skeleton key.

Like a sweetheart, some stories leave
without telling you why. Such is the case
for this one. Of course, you knew this was
coming. You know this story better than
your own.

ACKNOWLEDGMENTS

Without the friendship and dedication of the following people, this book would not exist in the form you see it here, and neither would I:

My incredible parents, Michael and Helen, and my brother, Rustin—I'm honored to be a member of "our club." The dear friends who generously served as early readers of this book: Evan, Monika, Kirk, George, Cassandra, Julie, Heather, S, and Wyatt. All the sweethearts of my past for helping me explore the strange cycles of love and loss— and for continuing to be good sports when I write about it. Marty McConnell/Vox Ferus for providing the writing prompt that somehow unfurled into an entire book. (Name an object. Name a body part. Now, replace the body part with the object . . .) The Shakespeare & Company bookshop in Paris for letting me sleep in the stacks as I chipped away at this poem. My brilliant editors at Ecco, Gabriella Doob and Daniel Halpern, and all the other talented people who went into making *Lumberjack* a physical, bound, real-life book: my copyeditor Susan Brown, designer Suet Yee Chong, production editor Dale Rohrbaugh, and publicist Martin Wilson. Beth Dial and all the other fine people at the National Poetry Series. And last, the incomparable Louise Glück, who gave this story a chance and made me feel that, for once, I was not writing into the void. Thank you.

The National Poetry Series was established in 1978 to ensure the publication of five collections of poetry annually through five participating publishers. The Series is funded annually by Amazon Literary Partnership, Betsy Community Fund, the Gettinger Family Foundation, Bruce Gibney, HarperCollins Publishers, Stephen King, Lannan Foundation, Newman's Own Foundation, News Corp, Anna and Olafur Olafsson, the O. R. Foundation, the PG Family Foundation, the Poetry Foundation, Laura and Robert Sillerman, Amy R. Tan and Louis De Mattei, Elise and Steven Trulaske, and the National Poetry Series Board of Directors.

THE NATIONAL POETRY SERIES WINNERS OF
2017 OPEN COMPETITION

The Lumberjack's Dove
GennaRose Nethercott
Chosen by Louise Glück for Ecco

Anarcha Speaks
Dominique Christina
Chosen by Tyehimba Jess for Beacon Press

feeld
Jos Charles
Chosen by Fady Joudah for Milkweed Editions

What It Doesn't Have to Do With
Lindsay Bernal
Chosen by Paul Guest for University of Georgia Press

Museum of the Americas
J. Michael Martinez
Chosen by Cornelius Eady for Penguin Books